THE FLUNG YOU

THE FLUNG YOU

LUCY ANDERTON

NEW MICHIGAN PRESS
TUCSON, ARIZONA

NEW MICHIGAN PRESS
DEPT OF ENGLISH, P. O. BOX 210067
UNIVERSITY OF ARIZONA
TUCSON, AZ 85721-0067

<http://newmichiganpress.com/nmp>

Orders and queries to nmp@thediagram.com.

Copyright © 2012 by Lucy Anderton.
All rights reserved.

ISBN 978-1-934832-36-3. FIRST PRINTING.

Printed in the United States of America.

Design by Ander Monson.

Cover image by Gabi Swiatkowska.

CONTENTS

Orange Hurts Me   1
if it is true that I eat electricity, then we   3
Not Something to be Captured. Did You See
   the Signs?   5
Close Catch   7
Lie Still, Lady Moth, In Our Wedlock Bed   8
With You   10
Toward the single point of slipping   11
On the Bus   13
still it looks   15
Shorn It Is: The Flung You.   16
The Beaten Moon   18
Carry the Heart   19
A Servant. A Hanging. A Paper House.   20
Suddenly: Fracture   22
fall #1   24
I'm sorry I have to put it this way, but   26
fall #2   28
and then she turned away   30
Broken. And Then. Once More.   31
bucket holds onto the flowers—battle the gush—
   bust the skin   34
fall #3   36
Is it Time to Give Up Yet? Should I Ask the Man?   38
fall #10   40

There are Teeth in the Egg   42
but also I have this fragment for you   44
Loss   45
on my knees   47

Acknowledgments   51

to my mother, Angharad Jones, my first you

*

and to my daughter, Ophélia Roux, my final you

Surely you stay my certain own, you stay my you.
 —Gwendolyn Brooks

ORANGE HURTS ME

    but I like it best. Cooling
out from a ruby tail—
unpools its hair over the edge
of the salt dawn lip…

    and into my most cindered nights, when I finally
weep, it is all orange—I see
you slide your eyelash
up to the roasting drops tripping
down my faded skin cheek.

    Or the fruit of those
paintings—served up sharp, almost scarlet:
it stabs through the soft snowy
paper, O tissue—you are such
trembled arms! Let me stare
until I am blind, until
there is nothing, nothing left—

    then sliced: humming
at your mouth, wet
glistening beads held
back by the tender tongueable skin, the pale
envelope, whispered cup, it rips

as I wed soaked up in red
silk and petal sliced with gold—
Yes, orange would take me
down. Uninvited, rose-orange
found its door through the candle
gleam flittering out off the crimson
satin feathers. That orange
is you. Walking away
against the thick, whitest snow.
The coldest April I knew.

IF IT IS TRUE THAT I EAT ELECTRICITY, THEN WE

are already in trouble. The stump
smoking in the furnace, blood

puffing up from the broken
bone. I crept along the bare face

corridor. At the core
of the wood, I felt it. In the thump

of the stoke and pile
it sat up on its pink haunches.

I've been taken up, taken up
in the fall of fire—I've taken

on fistfuls of sparks. Stinking
with reddening blossoms,

I've covered the night road
with my embarrassed body:

side-stepped and slung only this
old hair at the flank of the dark

bursting beast. Craned the neck
and polished the collar

bones—crushed the fair
fingers and pinched the tender

stem. There is a place
we step into—none too soft,

none too opening. It is there
that our silence waits. There

with its circling pace.

NOT SOMETHING TO BE CAPTURED. DID YOU SEE THE SIGNS?

As if I know what
    I'm doing—he marries

me. Did you hear that,
    yes, the line of dolls

hung up on the bush
    is too obvious? Rather

better: the spoon
    full of milk left alone

in the broken palm—the ghost
    song skidding out

the pane—in his arms I am
    still—but is *still* the best

way to beat this heart in-
    to ticking? My ring

finger aches—we know it
    is just winter knocking—and the swallows

agree that this hour is
    a fine one for freezing,

me? I've got glue to melt
    and reins to unbreak, mine

are needles dancing at top
    speed under the skin quilt—

pull it round you—I will
    shiver red and wakeful, but don't

ask me what
    is going on. It's better

if you keep your returned
    "I love you" to yourself—better

if I can let mine
    out into the faint

haze around you not
    to be answered, better

to wonder, emptying, so
    much better to wait—

CLOSE CATCH

Latch it on & then
the smoking hold.
Hatched easier: the spices
& the stones. Roam
the scent, you call it: that this:
odor: fold it up
in yours, melt it
bend it old
and sweat it bones & on
my knees. Yes. I sleep
like this unlaced
in the hot
fortune, unlinked &
sinking as love foxtrots
in all twist & turn
the furnace twinkles, twinkles up
O intimate lantern.
O standish cold.

LIE STILL, LADY MOTH, IN OUR WEDLOCK BED

Cheap wings don't make it
here. Duck

bites the moon
and escapes. There's

a broken fence
shining, the grease

from Rapunzel's hair
and hands never seemed

as long as that yet
yours reach me.

Shake. Spin
a rush of pinched

affections. Love.
Velour and the point

where cotton grew
from hands that picked

it. You old Daisy. We
loved each other once:

you were my sweet
heart and then a cloud

ate you. Quel Tango! Quel
Cocoon! Choked up

in ropes, a sparrow
strung its heart about

the branches in a wild
confusion of courtship.

There are juries for such
squabbles, and sweet, I

mean sweet, moments
in theatres. Slide over

here. Let me pull
the splinter from your

bite. You believe
me, don't you?

This old
oven heart?

WITH YOU

I am a stone.
Also, I am all heat
And simple

To break. Folded
Into you
I forget

Myself:
I become, become
Magnificent

Nothing, the flaming
Snow, the pale widow
Moon, a glass

Stung with nocturne, shy
And savage, held
To you.

TOWARD THE SINGLE POINT OF SLIPPING

In the slash of rain is a lamb
strung apart through a mess
of barbed wire.

And I saw it.
No.
I see her.
Red, wet guts,
and white.

The dogs not startled, hanging
barely at bay.

There is,
as you know, already nothing
to be done.

I am hiding.
From my father.
Up the mountain.
I am hidden
and the cries
overcome me.

No way to cut open
and run. We all

stumble: out
holding our dear
guts in our hands. And always

the teeth
that near and near.

And always the watchers
who do nothing.

Nothing now
to be done.

ON THE BUS

That silky
hair, black

and guided
into a slim

river down
her back was

all he could
see—won

dering if she
liked to have it

pulled back
hard and then

her head
when she

was being
fucked—she, turn

ing to look up
at his face,

skin tight
around his

mouth eyes
glistening

with something
ancient. Something

battered and
so ordinary.

STILL IT LOOKS

The air filled
now with eyes. Suddenly

a bird flies dead
into the pane
of a window.

I wait here.

Loosen, the Gaze.

I was wrong
about the night.

Unsolved.

SHORN IT IS:

Say: *Moon: it is a bitter pill*
She wrapped her parcel

between two healed fingers. Say: *she*
held her bucket

like a broken thrush beak—those heels
(you say) *what of sapphire*

the slate surfaces will give out
say: a moment has upstood

the stride of blood in my feet— has
leaves—pushed

in the stiff wind…You see that:
beat between us:

in your hands, the soft ribbon too.
at your teeth, a bowl

and a path for your fingers
clearly do not know

not the echo
though you are

THE FLUNG YOU.

stuck in God's throat and I will say:
in the cold air. It lay

triumphed, fooled us all—and I say: *she*
to her

sour in mud. And what of apple?
& drake? What do you think

when we look in to them? I cannot
in my jaw,

the empty tree been this too? Losing her
down her trunk

there is no dash, no comma to this
the spoon is settled

I'll wish this at you: an echo in glass
bright with sorries

to the soft place in this sleep. You
this self. You are

the odor, the lake.
it seems, you are.

THE BEATEN MOON

Immediately there is nudity.

O spoon edge, cut
through the cheek of the water drop.

From under his shirt
he pulls a bowl

packed with stars.

And the tails they left
when they splashed out

into our hair, that's when I knew
I do not wear champagne—

I cannot be
what the pearled bird
calls of me.

CARRY THE HEART

One boy wounds another boy.
Into the still air flies beat after beat: empty the heart.
Let the page carry these blossoms.
Let me turn out the fasting light.
Into the night-throat a blood owl tips a wail.
My own fingers won't rest at all.
Not even when I sleep:
that world where you are with me.

A SERVANT. A HANGING. A PAPER HOUSE.

I rose like a flannel

throat in a fire
of fog. Once an apple

biter—now gumming
ghost leavings. Wisps

of chambermaid keys blinking
through my lips. Entreat

the door knob— Silent,
but overused in the upstairs

sky. Fingerprints rushing
the wood. Jack hammer

wrists splintered & paralyzed.
Crack—& the tin pops

open—flooding out scarlet
seminary ribbons. Pausing

to notate a pregnant
wing. In the center

of a glittering scream
hangs an egg. Icy

& blue—left and that
is to say, I love you

and could you please
return to me

my tongue.

SUDDENLY: FRACTURE

It is lost, all of it
is also then found—hanging:
the suffering, shivering in brown

clumps off the bored
& wet sea post, holding there
like a slum of mussels:

dread: a lock grouting
out from the tight lip
of each shell. I knew it

when I set my foot
to the mourning floor—knew it
would waver in me

like an all-ways soaked flag.
Cradle up the pores:
a glass of boo-yah bloodied

and stank. Eggless
and soldered in shimmer.
Poor as the fly, dark

& stuck to a strip. O this tall
yawn. O this fear
pinched in the claws

of the hush-hush cat. I've gone
paler than that. Tripped
and fattered—toes

on their fairway
out of the mouth—
baby bending &

bending at the
waist—all ball
and soft—all and

never ready
for the soft blade
to skim us away

FALL #1

It must start again
through the slaughter

through the dark pond
of demerits. Daughter finds
her fingers ringing

with ice, with snow, with the lilt:
the fixed droplets—tend the bending

plant neck. Stay away
from the earth. We turn
to the earth. The spin

of her obstinate
skirts rush up the axel

of shred. When do the W's
stop. Lamp. Cradle. Dot.

Sypher. Crucifix. Bottle. Enter
the spoon. The bowl
is filled. Save the spit

for the ticket stubs and after
effects. When the window

wears a woman away is where
I will walk. Taxed

and without a real soul—
shoeless through the rain.
Ah yes—my surface

is
breaking with stain.

I'M SORRY I HAVE TO PUT IT THIS WAY, BUT

dear Herman, I am good here.
Camels walk about my sandy
bones. Also trees of licorice,
Kate Moss, and a wet corner
of the world that I cannot
name called my cunt. Herman, why
are you so called? Such a name
belongs only to old grey tires
—which by the way spoke to me—
I could not hear over the roar
of *Herman, Herman, Herman*—
their leather leaves now roasting
in the fire, their voices now
bleating at the blackness
that sheaths the slept-away day.
I trialed and traded carefully
cut curtains and long
delight-filled pisses on the side
of the country road for
a plumb fuck from you: Herman:
We shaking car window.
We traveling in the grille
of open smiles. Herman.
My spitting crater. I smoke
out the grasshoppers here
in the hammock—flat

on my broken back—my neck
en-throttled in the tender fist
clamp of the sun. I saw
one shadowy person here
in this snow Herman and
she spoke of you
with a red word or two
and I saw my tangle of whiteness—
that was slippered onto me
by these streets and cemetery
eyes. Here the birds two-step
rather than fly. Here Angela
Davis laughs in my float-
about face, my fist
held high. Here the wetness
will not come forth
in the cavern—the fleas
are drowning the pears
are waiting for their
silver green dive.

FALL #2

Sorghum saves the battle
and turns to the bath water

for that slow view of a bird
taking a turn past the pane.

Erudite—the only way to
fly in an oak tree's face. But

nature has no special
pair of gloves—and hooves

that I could never see
again what matters

is the crack of my neck bone
when I tilt my head for your perfect

kiss the mess will
will not leave me take it

now as this. Raise a bloodseed
to my lips and count on it:

I will drag my dirty dirty
tongue along. Broken

plates? And you did not
say you knew. Welcome

mat at the mouth way.
Trail pot of simple plant.

Wood in the cross hatch
slit at the door to the chill

house. I'm watching,
oh I'm watching your ass

move. The shake, though, that
is my sweet drop of stuff.

AND THEN SHE TURNED AWAY

or was it because she turned
away? She turned away, she

turned her head away. Her back
upon the stairs, her body
on her back, her body just

above mine, just above
beneath. She shimmered there,
she shook, she shook

a silent spot in me & then
she turned her head, her
gaze, away, so what

could I do
but love
her?

BROKEN. AND THEN. ONCE MORE.

So as to stay, I must
come. But without you

where am I coming to? Alone

my coming breaches an awful
floating up, up, unhinged

then—no, don't turn away. There:

a picture of a child.
There the child, but no longer

the child with an untouched waist

or wrist. She looks past
to the park. No one is there.

Every single thing is there.

The soft mud under the brisk, green,
shadowless advance, you can't call

them fingertips, you can,

though, I do. I don't
like the word *bed*

even for myself. Better

the carpet rubs my back
raw. Or the cement edging

the fake pool blue

where Fiorenzo did his knees in,
my young knobby spine. You see?

The legions I float? *To stay*

*I must come. But come where
without you?* To say that

I must fasten my self to

a thing called pleasure
but not pleasure, no, not, no

center but the falling

of lashes of fibers…the circle,
it thickens around me.   If

I throw my arms straight

up, I am an edge, a slim ghost.
My arms out? I am your shade

looking to join with your

own un-eased skin. How
do I say, to stay I must

unthread the snaps, wear

the daisy chain, push pink
back under my skirt, sit still, keep

the elbows not for battery,

bounding, mustard
will crease in the sun

beneath my bruising hand—don't

let that lead you to the idea
of secrets. It's a long melting

thing, a ribbon? Yes. No,

I can't see it, it's untangling
through the key hole—here, bend

down now, see? That's me—never

stopped, digging the grave
where the water stands to swim.

BUCKET HOLDS ONTO THE FLOWERS— BATTLE THE GUSH—BUST THE SKIN

open but softly, with the tongue
of a long thin-necked note—there

are things we cannot help
but traipse through, red flecks

on our cheeks and the stop
of a car on a long dark street

as I did that night you took back
your open throat, the ground

was cold and I was in love
with my death again like

some stupid there
Sylvianne and there

was dust in my teeth. Against the black
jaw of roadway, these poor hands

sprang out, beggars, two
petrified stars—and a small stone

began its suffocation at the base
of my neck. Body/tunnel. Spirit/

bridge. The silver bells twinkled
up the night. Immediately

there is silence: And how severe
each back can be. The nail

of a crushed finger, the lash
of a closing lid, the wings of the moth

flying hot into that glass sun,
the bones of a body, or

more like, the thin stem
of a plant.

FALL #3

Isn't it just a crack
in the jaw. Displeasure
turns at the clock. Vessel
of turbulence. Center

of wide moated absolution.

The Longing.

In the middle of the night
a craft arrives: skimming
the true liquid dream
and you are in it! Your face!
Is all the time changed—
but you know you're the same
one who hides in the cloak
of those others with their bitten notes.

I will never love anyone else—

you tell me

I won't. I believe it.

The arbitration between stone and petal.

Clapped on the one. Found
favor with the two. I withdrew
my promise of a careful
cup of tea. Give me something

onto which I may hold…is
what they say. Goliath
held everything—David
let it all fly. May the die
fall, the cards do their tip-topple,
the picked on crayons
melt with joy in that final
fat sun. I am no more done

with the swath of crinkled
cloth then I am
with you—my
once more feathered Lamb.

IS IT TIME TO GIVE UP YET? SHOULD I ASK THE MAN?

With the pale yellow
                honey comb? I am
                                    so white? I am

  transparent. In my room
  the words thistle. I won't

speak here. Here
                the bees were a long
                                smoke pushing out

  of the bubbling wax?
  Here there is a song—

yes, now, even song
        is too much. Now look—when
                          you put me on the corner

  with a coin in my small
  palm, you knew I would

take the first bus to come.
        Here the wheel swerves.
                          Here you are a bird call

    sounding when I refuse
    to wake. Is it time

yet? Can I give up?
                      I want to be ready. Turn
                                    up the sunlight. Hanging

    out to dry there is the list.
    It is a tubular thing.

Stickiness is your third
             voice—and between my fingers—
                            just the red, red stain.

FALL #10

Lamp the long night through.
I was sleeping=didn't you see me

there with a birdling running
through my mouth? Holding

the camouflage has always
been a thatched leaf dance—oh you

proper actor, you clover, you potted
rolling hill—I am no cat

in the face of your butterfully—no
paper butterscotching your ink.

The pinion courts the justice, seeds
the cage, scents the hot summer bee

and there we both stand
in the plaza, mud and pearl

our cathedral bodies
sparrowing out and away and apart,

sand in our sad hands.
In your sweet boat I found

both the flight and the can't
swim. I choose this not-rock,

with its not-grassy gaze—I choose
this ocean, I give you land's end.

THERE ARE TEETH IN THE EGG

Drying up is never
easy. Sloppy

with glitter. (I caught
the holy horn
by the cow—opened

the stickler ribs
and found no heart

but how it was down
to me and the snap
of fear in your chest.)

Stare at those shivering
shoulders—you

won't move to cover
your golden
ankles, no

one wants that—
come on now—

sever that stink
from your hip—slip
into a cup of ruby

red hiccup
and eyelash

bats for the mothers
in the stands
to reason—no one

loves a pearl
with grit

in its teeth—
a slit in its
back—get up

from the slack
puddle of daze,

take the bird—yes
break its straw
neck—funny

to find that
within you.

BUT ALSO I HAVE THIS FRAGMENT FOR YOU

Even now I see the pocket. I see how
we will end. How we will begin. And how
I will lose everything

>   and at dawn. It will be Dawn. I will section
>   off my limbs on that old black road.

I will sleep it into blood.

LOSS

—*Untranslatable!*—you
whispered. Untrans-
latable: That shove

off course— like ink
into milk. Like dementia
in the cold

shoes of soldiers. Now: hack
off a scrap of
lightening—string

it about your ankle
bone: You say: Under
ground level we are

all the click of knuckle
loosened to wood—ready
for the crush

of night—the fall, yes,
the falling and then
the push—that gasp

will catch us
too late: You say: To say
Despair is thin—

this said while we watch
that pigeon
stepping, stepping

in the road
a circle round her
soft dying mate.

ON MY KNEES

pleading
has nothing

to do with knocks on the chin.
there are women and men

who know this. fold it
into newspapers. drop it

in drinking water.
wait

like gravestones
to be asked. waiting

grows you
roots

spreads bark
up your legs

cracks fistfuls of twigs
from the eyelids

of your wrists,
leaves you

waving in wind
songs, agreeing

with trees
that to say

      Anything!   *I will do*   *Anything!*

is
to throw

your arms
round

a fracture
in the stars.

ACKNOWLEDGMENTS

Tremendous gratitude to the editors who decided to previously publish the following poems. Thanks also and always to the Virginia Center for the Creative Arts for time, space, food, and France. Finally, I am indebted to Ander Monson and the fine staff at New Michigan Press and *DIAGRAM* for their steadfast dedication to exploring and putting forward writing in a myriad of forms, and for their generous choice to publish these poems as a collection.

AGNI Online—"On the Bus"
American Letters & Commentary—"There are Teeth in the Egg"
Barrelhouse Magazine—"if it is true that I eat electricity, then we"
Barrow Street Review—"still it looks"
Beloit Poetry Journal—"Toward the single point of slipping" & "I'm sorry to have to put it this way, but"
Born Magazine—"A Servant. A Hanging. A Paper House."
Crazyhorse—"Not Something to be Captured. Did You See the Signs?" & "Close Catch"
DIAGRAM—"Loss" & "fall #3"
Forklift, Ohio—"With You"
From The Fishouse— "On the Bus"
The Iowa Review—"A Servant. A Hanging. A Paper

House." & "Lie Still, Lady Moth, In Our Wedlock Bed"

Tarpaulin Sky—"fall #1"

Union Station Magazine—"bucket holds onto the flowers—battle the gush—bust the skin" & "Broken. And Then. Once More"

Verse Daily—"Not Something to be Captured. Did You See the Signs?"

Wicked Alice—"on my knees"

COLOPHON

Text is set in a digital version of Jenson, designed by Robert Slimbach in 1996, and based on the work of punchcutter, printer, and publisher Nicolas Jenson.

There was a road, and LUCY ANDERTON crossed it. There were doors that she opened and those she left closing. Once she said "No" to a second helping of peas (but only once). No rabbit ever dropped from the beak of hawk to land upon her head while she rode a motorbike. Although that happened to someone she loves. She has held onto your hand. She may never know your own sweet face. Babies were lost. Lucy was not one of them. These are things that make any biography. Lucy also chases after the knowing of that which does not.

NEW MICHIGAN PRESS, based in Tucson, Arizona, prints poetry and prose chapbooks, especially work that transcends traditional genre. Together with DIAGRAM, NMP sponsors a yearly chapbook competition.

DIAGRAM, a journal of text, art, and schematic, is published bimonthly at THEDIAGRAM.COM. Periodic print anthologies are available from the New Michigan Press at NEWMICHIGANPRESS.COM/NMP.

www.ingramcontent.com/pod-product-compliance
Lightning Source LLC
Chambersburg PA
CBHW031501040426
42444CB00007B/1170